Once in Blockadia

Also by Stephen Collis

Poetry
Anarchive
The Commons*
DECOMP (with Jordan Scott)
Mine
On the Material*
To the Barricades*

Fiction
The Red Album

Nonfiction
Dispatches from the Occupation: A History of Change*
Phyllis Webb and the Common Good: Poetry /
    Anarchy / Abstraction*
Reading Duncan Reading: Robert Duncan and the
    Poetics of Derivation
Through Words of Others: Susan Howe and
    Anarcho-Scholasticism

Available from Talonbooks

Once in Blockadia

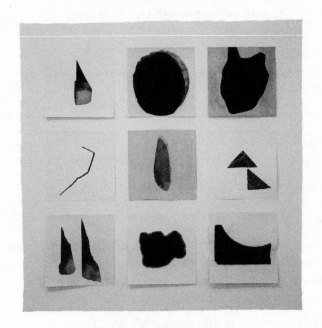

STEPHEN
COLLIS

Talonbooks

Talonbooks
278 East First Avenue, Vancouver, British Columbia, Canada V5T 1A6
www.talonbooks.com

First printing: 2016

Typeset in Freight Text
Printed and bound in Canada on 100% post-consumer recycled paper

Interior and cover design by Typesmith
Cover art by Genevieve Robertson, *River Catalogue* (2015), found bitumen, gouache, and charcoal.

Talonbooks gratefully acknowledges the financial support of the Canada Council for the Arts, the Government of Canada through the Canada Book Fund, and the Province of British Columbia through the British Columbia Arts Council and the Book Publishing Tax Credit.

Library and Archives Canada Cataloguing in Publication

Collis, Stephen, author
        Once in blockadia / Stephen Collis

Poems.
ISBN 978-1-77201-015-2 (paperback)

        I. Title.

PS8555.O4938O53 2016   C811'.54   C2016-904639-7

CONTENTS

Our spread over the earth was fuelled by...
incessantly burning whatever would burn...
From the earliest times, human civilization
has been no more than a strange luminescence
growing more intense by the hour...

—W. G. SEBALD

Blockadia is not a specific location on a map
but rather a roving transnational conflict zone
that is creeping up with increasing frequency
and intensity wherever extractive projects are
attempting to dig and drill...

—NAOMI KLEIN

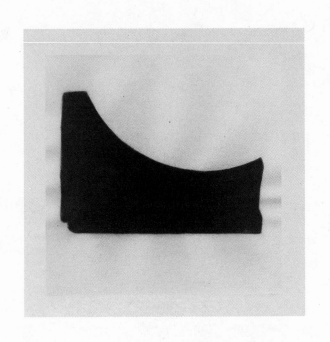

Subversal

THE COURT TRANSCRIPT

We got hella people, they got helicopters.
—THE COUP

BC Supreme Court Transcripts, November 5 2014, Submissions for the plaintiff:

So the evidence is that on October 28th an encampment had been put in place at borehole number 2. Now, you'll recall that borehole number 2 is right by Centennial Way, so it's the most easily accessible part of the park. By 11:00 p.m. there were four to six people at borehole number 2, but more significantly there was a tent and cars surrounding the tent and the location of borehole number 2. Later that afternoon additional people had congregated around borehole number 2. There were more cars and it has become the centre point of the events. And you'll see some pictures of some video where there is now a large encampment completely blocking any access anyone could have to the park from that point, and specifically to borehole number 2, and it involves people, temporary structures and cars; ironically, all in breach of the Burnaby bylaws, among other laws.

So on October 29th the plaintiff dispatched employees and contractors to three separate locations to perform work: Barnet Marine Park adjacent to Barnet Highway, as I've described, borehole number 1, borehole number 2. The work intended to be performed at borehole number 1 and 2 was to erect posts and signage to mark as work zone for upcoming work related to the drilling of boreholes.

At borehole number 1 a platform must be erected and a drilling rig installed for the purpose of drilling the borehole. It must be fenced and secure for operation and safety reasons, and the intention was to start that process.

At borehole number 2 a mobile drilling platform will be used. It will be driven onto the site. That area too must be secured and fenced for operational safety purposes.

So what occurred was at borehole number 1 when the crew tried to access it they encountered a number of protesters who congregated in and around the site. They physically blocked access to the borehole, shouted slogans of variety — and I'll take you through the affidavits in a moment — behaved in a manner that made it clear to the crew that if they attempted to perform the tasks for which they came on site there would be a physical confrontation. They would be physically prevented from doing so.

So you'll see the pictures show a variety of people arm in arm physically creating a fence or a barrier between the crew and what was borehole number 1. It appears that there's some sort of structure erected at borehole number 1 as well. There's a white tarp. And so that attempt eventually was abandoned, and I'll describe that conduct.

The same crew went by borehole number 2, but you'll see from the affidavits they acknowledge they knew they weren't going to get there because of what they knew was there. But they went by it to see and to try and didn't even attempt.

So I'd like to take you through the material that is exhibit S through BB. So exhibit S is a *Burnaby News Leader* article that involves, among other things, an interview with the defendant Collis, and from other affidavit evidence identifying him at various locations, that is him in the picture. You can see a group calling themselves "the caretakers" says they:

... will do what we can to hinder Kinder Morgan from accessing two sites on Burnaby Mountain.

The description was the work that's required. The reference to the City of Burnaby already trying to block from proceeding:

... but on Thursday the National Energy Board issued an order granting Kinder Morgan access. On Friday the company submitted its required 48-hour notice.

And then Mr. Collis is not quoted, but referenced as saying that Kinder Morgan will have to go through his band of citizen rangers. A reference to the camp that's being built along Centennial Way. A reference that Mr. Collis was at the camp on Monday. And then over a page a quote from him saying:

Collis says the group's intent is to be in the way of Kinder Morgan accomplishing its work.

And then a description of what's occurred:

Erected a tent over the spot where borehole number 2 is supposed to be drilled onto the mountain. It's surrounded by a hodgepodge assembly of tree branches, discarded building materials, like boards, a sheet of plexiglas, even an old mattress, computer keyboard and plastic Polaroid camera. It's decorated with bright orange safety vests as well as a couple of jack-o-lanterns with "Stop Kinder Morgan."

And I won't take you to the Burnaby bylaws, but it's obviously refuse, in breach of the bylaw. And Mr. Collis describes this as:

This is visual. This is an obstacle.

He is referenced as saying:
Members of the group have been erecting and manning the encampment for a few weeks.

I'm quite aware, My Lord, that these are not direct quotes from Mr. Collis. There is evidence I will take you through where he says these things directly. He's posted a YouTube — I'll call it interview, if you will, where much of what is here is confirmed. And so then exhibit T is a website called "Beating the Bounds," which is actually a website maintained by Mr. Collis, and so the first page is the "About" page where it references occasional notes, and then one of the notes posted is a note that on the website talks about the last barrel of oil on Burnaby Mountain.

Sometimes the world narrows to a very fine point, a certain slant of light, the head of a needle you need to pass through. I don't care right now about the National Energy Board of Canada, merely a corporate tool for shoehorning global energy projects into other people's territories, a funnel for money from the public to the private sector. I don't care about this or that court of law, appeals and constitutional challenges. I don't care about the drones, unmarked cars or CSIS agents. I don't even care that much about the rain.

And then flip over the page:

> I care about the people who have come together
> to stand in the forest on a mountain in the
> path of a pipeline.

And he describes why he cares about them. And
the next paragraph:

> As has been our intention all along, we will
> occupy public land, a city park, and prevent
> Kinder Morgan from carrying out its destructive
> work, work opposed by local First Nations,
> opposed by the City of Burnaby and opposed by
> the majority of Burnaby residents. While the
> case goes back and forth in the courts, our
> intention is to keep Kinder Morgan wrapped
> up dealing with us, either until a court
> somewhere sides with the people against this
> mega-corporation or until the NEB's December
> 1 deadline for KM's complete application.

He describes his views about protecting the
local environment, and then on the bottom:

> As barricades were assembled from garbage
> dumped down a hillside from a parking lot in
> Burnaby Mountain ... an old rusted oil barrel
> was uncovered and rolled up the hill. It's a
> talisman, a symbol of the old world we are
> trying to resist and change. It is, we hope,
> the last oil barrel that will have anything
> to do with this mountain forest.

So underneath the poetry is a description of
how the barricade was constructed.

THIRTEEN TREES

A raven announces territory
As deep distancing echo
Gnome's are not seen
But they are evening
Shadow on mountain trail
Black bears amble to
Forage beneath blue
Heavens above clearing
Where thirteen trees lie
On forest floor and thirteen
Shadows still hold up the sky
Holding off the helicopter world
Dropping – bituminous – in their midst

Territory shadows helicopters
Lines strewn shadows for
Lines of piped fire fused
Earth water stream bears
The dead singing sad songs
At abandoned mills still seen
As somebody's capital no not
Some *body* but portfolio or like
How the absence of money can be
Bundled bought and sold as trees
Shadow those bodies not bodies
But ossifying metabolic processes housing
Actual liquid moments of arboreal bliss

Ravens hone tree sound from
Gnome's Home Trail then
Coloured graphs of Fukushima
Tendrils crossing the Pacific
Each step helicopters us closer
To turn ocean dumps ourselves
Decaying animals tell the market
Hands off everything or opt
Out of opting out again
And throw metallurgy after
Scant agency or renewed animality
Rattle cry bray at the dark edges
Afire and together as trees shadows as sound

If bears arrived in helicopters
Or ravens had thirteen ways
Of marking rupture though
I am not the graphite in your
Pencil William Wordsworth
Though graphite is one of the most
Refined hydrocarbons and was
Mined in the heart of your lakes
Fuelling the march of privileged
Beauty as in Titian's painting
Each body finds its own light
Source and only the two cheetahs
Are as dark as ensnared Bacchus

Underneath the poetry
Not just description but the act
The biotariat at borehole 1 and 2
Ravens and bears last *Kinder* last
Morgan or imagine pipes collapsing
Beneath re-Indigenized streets
Black once pulsing veins of some
Carboniferous leviathan and
Not a single car on the roads
Everyone having forgotten
The practice of speed in isolation
Taking instead to small crystalline streams
To catch water striders in outstretched palms

Dear accomplice we
Will be as children tomorrow
We will prune shared gardens
No flowers will field us oysters
The times will be incipient
A chorus of shared groans will
Mark all our small tragedies
No one will see the eyes
We do not possess
We will not repatriate value
Value will be the heat in our hands
As we reach out to another
And pull them onto the common shore

Shapeless future
We steal away
Far from press releases
To fish on damp rocks
To one side of the nothing
Power does not already control
Practising another mode
Of gasping – intake stardust
Infinitesimal drops of pure water
Oil don't burn tomorrow's children
Oil by turns turned out swoon
Turning spheres colours green water
Turning blue sail turning out clean air

BLOCKADIA

Beneath the poetry the barricade beneath sandstorms digital trading beneath our selves the ones we have been waiting for beneath our allies manufactured enemies beneath casual parks formal profits beneath the review process other possible futures beneath resignation new uplift beneath deals betrayal beneath the singularity of owning the multitude of needing beneath the human voice the systemic response beneath government real abstractions beneath a trial an error beneath graphed assessments the particularity of soils beneath media the feel of our hands beneath the outflow of resources the influx of commodities beneath the right to exclude the right not to be excluded beneath the drill platform the mountain beneath litigants lovers beneath the bees little rockets.

Then we were all engines. Someone asked, how will you get to work or wherever? Like the possible was always equivalent to the available. We were not only saying no. Was it really so strange to decolonize on camera? Only if the *Sun* news reporter tells you to GET A JOB. Nobody likes it but what are you going to do about it. Machine says, no cross *this* line. It doesn't happen all at once – it is between the frames and it is internal to the social process of collective individuation and it is a firefly lit in the dark and it is ongoing in the soil, perc and leach field, mushroom explosion at borehole number 1. We are engines of change, component parts, aqueducts. NGOs mansplaining at the police line, someone said they mounted a cavalcade of photo-op arrests. That's harsh – we all wanted to delete certain processes – to say *fuck this* under or over our varied breaths, smile at bypass of yellow tape, sacred fire. What is Carboniferous after all? The engines behind the blockade were carved cedar, raven-winged, and reached as militant flesh across the metabolic rifts we were – back in time and forward in time, lifting material from the forest to be a barrier to human stupidity.

First there were two or three. Then there were a few more searching among trees in the park. Then there were more than the 13 trees cut down for seismic testing. We were growing in a forest on a mountain, mushrooms or mitochondria. And bear and deer and raccoon. Underneath the canopy, the bestiary. A pipe could not be put through – predatory – or for pretext – was our mandate. Question: what is horizontal directional drilling anyway? Answer: depends on how deep you imagine unceded goes – bedrock and beyond? Then there were more than 31 and then there were more than 301. The barricade was made more from people and what transpired between people and more people than it was the junk hauled out of the woods and piled at the borehole. And bear and deer and raccoons and ravens. Maybe we were animals coming to the nearness of other animals releasing a social hormone or howl or moan and attracting us and others sensing this and howling or moaning back. And children and grandmothers and queers and punks. Then there were more and more or really just barely enough in the end which was no end or resolution. Morning under tarps blue light was sublime congress. Evening and ghost cars and drones did not dissuade. I will forever recall walking through yellow wood towards a horizon not of this world that is of this world that was passed person to person invisible like solidarity until each person was full of this thing that was tomorrowing when cops and courts and coordinates intervened as systems of public doubt and private accumulation.

It's true we were consumers in a largely affluent society who work for wages and use these wages to purchase consumer goods and thereby sometimes derive enjoyment and certainly our continued material existence precarious and dependent same but different. Who have for instance purchased automobiles which run on fossil fuels to drive perhaps to the store or perhaps on a vacation over sharp-terrained coastal mountains to peer into pristine lakes or possibly spot a bear upslope and loping away into a stand of second-growth fir. Who run errands in those automobiles that are of ambiguous import and usefulness and who bring home large amounts of petroleum-based products containing chemically processed foods and amusements we will soon dispose of. Who also have mobile phones perhaps to text a friend that are very distracting and amusing and which are also made of petroleum-based products and also contain rare earth metals extracted in disparate parts of the planet and brought to us by ships and trucks also powered by fossil fuels so we may play perhaps *Plants vs. Zombies*. Who did not necessarily mean to do anything harmful but fell for the sleekness of products and the way marketing made everything seem sexy and easy and convenience became a truism almost no one could contradict now isn't that convenient but for whom and what structures of profiteering and oppression lie beneath the chemicals rocketing at the hives we keep?

And so I think about barricades: the barricade as apparent threat, the barricade as unfathomable assertion, the barricade as the unwanted obstacle that stretches to its limits the tenuous fantasy of settler belonging. What if we instead understood the barricade – both as a physical barrier and as a practice of symbolic signification – less as an obstacle and threat, and more as something erected to protect "all of us"? ... As sites of seemingly irreconcilable conflict between Indigenous and non-Indigenous communities, the barricade is mistaken in the mainstream as the violent embodiment of this impasse rather than an opportunity for its transcendence. After all, there is no violence inherent to the barricade itself; its threat stems from its capacity to highlight the violence inherent in the colonial nation-state. Like the example of the Buffalo Commons map, then, the barricade could provide an opening onto a different relationship to land and to one another – one that both acknowledges the violence of settlement and resource extraction, and that affirms shared obligations to care-take the land for the wellbeing of future generations.

—ALLISON HARGREAVES AND DAVID JEFFERESS

The future has never meant so much to us. Science graphs ever more exacting projections of limit and overshoot. We can no longer claim an unwitting accidentalism. Like adopters of Watt's steam engine thinking they just might improve production a smidge with this smouldering sea-coal contraption. Or so the story goes, all the fossil apostles of nascent fossil capital. Trees growing thickly, thick with bark, lignin emporium, three hundred million years ago, just a carbon blink. Crushed and entombed till the black rock flakes fire, or the liquid aquifers of burnable formerness ooze darkling beneath bog and peat. *Burn out the day, burn out the night.* A decades-long straw our grandchildren extend back to us, sucking our air through to their depleted days, their collapsible-lung laughter, their voices barely audible, crackling back dry as fire. Or an *underground pipeline we got our breath back through.* The transition to fossil fuels was as much about power as it was about *power.* The body electric and the body politic. The need to discipline labour. So fossil fuels fanned class-war flames – the struggle over power (energy) was a power (social) struggle – maybe we had the right idea when we smashed the machines after all, Ned. Now they surveil and curtail us through a present of no more transitions, no more alternatives too. Clip our speech into their guns running empty. Glyphs on what were once oil barrels marked as toxic as tears. Beer-can pinhole cameras lay siege to their pipeline projects with dim night-vision oratories and ghost-tree appliques. The campus is just over the hill, or used to be. The fire started when we decided to farm tanks on its forest slopes.

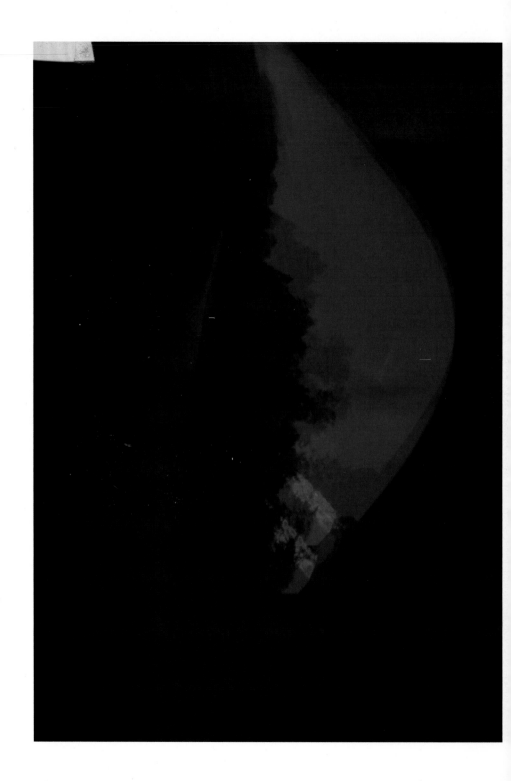

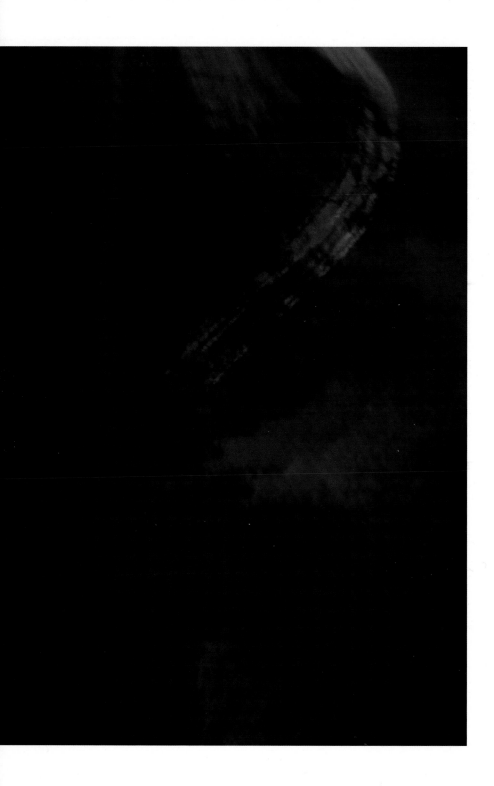

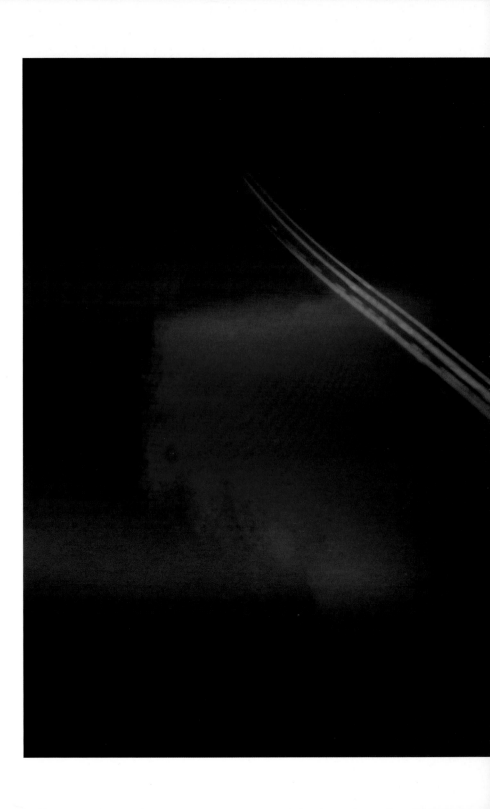

Watch a documentary called *Oil Across the Rockies*. Quote it was logical that a pipeline be run to the sea end quote. Safe under the ground of 1953. To the seaport right-of-way carved round spectacular slopes above Fraser River banks. Banks and forms of value. Right of way. Engineers studied aerial photographs tramped through woods above the river. Arrangements for easements. Right of way. Is no right. It's blistering listening to this. Riverbanks swept clear of timber and Aboriginal title. Banks rights safe underground unquestioned. According to the pressure it would have to withstand. Safe underground beneath the poetry. Ditching machines the pressure it would have to. Took small streams in their stride. Welded tied-in and doused in hot coal tar. Top padding of soft earth. Over bodies not mentioned tombs. A section pulled across the river dredge and laid at Port Mann fifteen feet below the riverbed the pressure. Quote like a fabulous serpent it slithered into the depths end quote. Moments when everything looked hopeless and valves and valves and valves and. Into the depths augured well for economic progress fiction method. Lush growths of grain over subterranean artery of oil. Safe under ground. Security lie breach surveil radical hole cut oil fire heat drought hole radical dupe dump oil. Fictitious economic method it was logical said method said bank. I wanted to watch the next video cued: *Radioactive Wolves of Chernobyl*. Fur coat private capital bought paid lush paid hole photo-op continent burnt sold fire wolf howl sold future hole melts.

Shell Oil has been using scenario planning *to explore the future* since the early 1970s. What future what exploration unknown. Shell's *futurists* develop *what if* scenarios of *plausible futures* in order to make their business plans more – socially palatable. *What if* more of the same is no plan is stuck system. These plans have increasingly come to accept climate change as a *plausible* future factor. Apparently, a future without the market's dripping black wings is not – plausible. Futurists are investors. Time is money. A thick coat of seeming choice applied, of seeming change applied to feathered dark aperture. *Help Shell change the world* the gas pump LED crawls menace force menace distraction. What world and what change unknown ungraphable and a pause in the plausible as we warm to no ideas.

There are only two scenarios, when it comes down to it: **Scramble** and **Blueprint**. They map conceptually a suicidal free-for-all fight for the last remaining planetary resources, or a planned and careful diversification of a varied fossil-fuel portfolio as a response to civil-society pressure to curb carbon emissions. We can do this the easy way, or the hard way – the choice is yours.

After Malcolm Lowry's Dollarton shack burned down in 1944, destroying along with it his manuscript of *In Ballast to the White Sea*, he is said to have sat looking across Burrard Inlet, bottle in hand, to where the **Shell Oil** refinery's sign blinked on and off, its neon "**S**" burnt out so that the word **hell** was left to intermittently light up the night sky.

Walking the route of the pipeline through suburban Burnaby we observed streams filled with spring runoff and yellow high-pressure pipeline warning signs standing midstream yellow reflectors cautioning raccoons. The view down Shellmont past the tank farm, towards Burnaby Lake. Suburban street march strangeness though only one passing driver gave us the finger. Kinder Morgan's Trans Mountain pipeline carries product for Shell and other companies from Alberta to the coast. "Kinder Morgan" might be translated from approximate German as "tomorrow's children." ET IN BLOCKADIA EGO. *Sous les pavés, la plage.* It was always what was under the poetry that mattered. Who said I said this wasn't a court it was a forest they wanted to drill a pipeline through mountain replacing a pipeline near mountain we said no now who knows what will result. We had our own **blueprints** had to **scramble** to avoid traffic at Duthie and Hastings just beneath the university above the pipeline beneath our feet territory beneath map the barricades still an imagined possibility in the path of imagined new pipelines a radium wolf in the mind and raccoons carrying red flags we sang we homed a long line making a circle to begin.

Forest perambulations existed since at least the time of Magna Carta. They were ceremonial walks about a territory for asserting and recording its boundaries, that is, "beating the bounds." A perambulation was a kind of peripatetic map, or walkabout, in which briar-scratched skin, stubbed toes, aching legs aided the memory… The perambulation of the New Forest authorized by Charles II in 1671 resulted in a Latin document that, translated, comprises a single sentence over six pages long, of approximately one thousand nine hundred and eighty words, many hundreds of prepositional phrases (the grammatical unit most having to do with position and direction) – to, from, by, beyond, across, in – and human and natural landmarks – ditch, post, hedge, vale, pond, gate, rover, oak, beech, grave, croft, marsh, lane, road, ford – with current name, alias, former names, thus making the text layered with semantic history and compact with minute orientation.

—PETER LINEBAUGH
The Magna Carta Manifesto

Walking the route of the proposed new pipeline still an imaginary line in data bank accounts begin on river mud banks beneath bridge the pilings & log booms small midspan island treed & reedy temporary trail closed signs barbed-wire hypocrisy of man-made habitats in shadow of cathedralled concrete bridge towers we counter-surveil with beer-can pinhole camera under cottonwood trees unstable popweed & pizza boxes & rebar & rebar & rebar the dirt banks of heavily worked earth through trespass fencing past vending garage doors industrial park polymer shapes stacked Coke machines behind fencing Schnitzer Cat Leavitt the nest of yellow & blue crane arms at Phoenix Truck & Crane then daisies clover bees all the blackberry brambles fit to neglect along United Boulevard other side of Lafarge gravel pit aggregate trucks Coke & Wendy's Crystal Brite with daisy & share the road sign by the waist-high grass turning onto Schooner just two blocks before the imagined new route leaves the old past Home Depot Subway & the inflatable Elvis at Kia Motors we tie another beer-can pinhole camera to surveil the would be as we are surveilled too at the Coquitlam Transfer Station Fraser Mills blackberry heaps & highway noise & heat winners history losers story we tell the landfill along the thousands of power poles piled between United & the Fraser moving west past train whistle dumps & junk space wildflowers then down along access road trespassing to the Brunette River alder & cottonwood & brambles without end shopping cart in the river storm drain pump station & so to the train tracks rust fragments old but active trestle we cross webs beneath weed scorn & junk heap lesions near giant LED screen jutting over raised roadway & so to Braid Station river train tracks access road park trail & possible pipeline all following same ragged cut through suburban landscape blackberries follow too.

Think of Stanley Kubrick's 1964 film *Dr. Strangelove or: How I Learned to Stop Worrying and Love the Bomb* and the idea of the "doomsday machine" – something once triggered cannot be turned off, no matter how brainless we set our destruction in motion. Originally, the film was supposed to end with a pie fight in the U.S. War Room. Just before which the barely reformed Nazi Dr. Strangelove (played brilliantly by Peter Sellers) proposes a **scenario** in which a select few and eugenically chosen humans are preserved in deep mine shafts until the nuclear winter is over (in about a hundred years, give or take, he suggests). Just in case the Soviets have the same idea, and sneak a bomb into *their* mine shaft, General Turgidson (played by George C. Scott) recommends the remnants of the American portion of the human race (the most powerful men and most "stimulating" women) take a bomb or two beneath ground with them – to avoid a potential future "mine-shaft gap."

This is wolf leap run wolf calm exterior. Not apparatus not proven. Like carbon capture which is bunk theory wherein waste carbon might be stored in abandoned mine shafts has no chance no scenario Doctor. Like we could not even like liking the project Rodrigo. It's up to us building forges building links. This wolf love not strange love not hidden camera wolf cold howl irradiate cesium. Sit in the woods and wait it is autumn it is trading. **Tsilhqot'in** says *it is collective title and cannot be encumbered in ways that would prevent future generations from using or enjoying it* means we all must cede to the unceded home to unsettle settling. Pipefitters. Markets. Title. Out sharp camp Indigenous forest home blockade home territory not lost come wolves run wolves come leap becquerel leap along path no pipeline has or will be built circling haven glow remorse no remorse breathe deep air touch fertile land roaming.

Scenario: in the contaminated exclusion zone or "zone of alienation" around a crippled nuclear reactor "forests, marshes and fields teem with activity." The "ill-fated reactor has not created a desert, but a lush wilderness"; "remnant orchards are harvested by wild boars" and "ruins drown in waves of green." Now the "years of cultivation" by human beings appear as "only a temporary inconvenience" for the other species now fluorescing once again. White-tailed eagle, peregrine falcon, dormice, deer, wild boar, bison, wild horse, wolves, beavers, otters – "for humans, this land is lost," but for other species – despite radiation – "this ecosystem is in robust health." Beaver dams return the Pripyat marshes to their original extent, flooding former farms. Eight-foot catfish haunt the cooling ponds near the disabled reactor. The wolves may be radioactive, but they are as prolific as in other reserves returning fire.

Scenario: an architectural firm proposes the "development of infrastructure elements" to "facilitate tourism" in the contaminated exclusion zone around a nuclear reactor that suffered a meltdown decades ago. "We suggest the following types of tourism: extreme, industrial, ecological, game tourism, and photo-safari." Diagrams: "death zone" = sad face; "life zone" (icons for scientist, horse, and Neanderthal-like tourist with camera around neck and dollar sign) = happy face. At the core of the proposal is an "environmentally friendly" monorail "covered with a thick layer of metal protecting people from radioactive exposure and excessive sun radiation." "Old objects located in the area are regarded as tourist attractions." I can see all the way to never from here. "The proposed solutions will transform the abandoned territory which is now financed at the expense of the taxpayers into a prosperous tourist destination."

Don't project meteors and blight don't forest our French havens our proto-revolutionary profits only one kind of liberty to sell for climate's half-life I come upon money in low hollows as a gas it glows lucent with epiphenomenal ooze triggers Geiger clicks market share glow I might migraine my way to opacity still might will killing sprees or spending sprees absence fluoresce resident species strange love radio wolf active wolf radio home strange because it was there because it was unpolluted and unproductive because money not waste not want not double down death double don't climate quote my anger for instrumental use don't species this dream don't drain it of beaver weight get access to bunk meritocracy get excess and milk it white make zombie market future make it now.

Surveyor: Belike you think it free for you to censure other men at your pleasure, and to judge them after your own vain conceit, and yet no reply must take hold of your vain quarrel, that riseth of mere malice against the innocent.

Farmer: Innocent? How can that be, when you pry into men's Titles and estates, under the name (forsooth) of Surveyors, whereby you bring men and matter in question often times, that would (as long time they have) lie without any question. And often times you are the cause that men lose their Land; and sometimes they are abridged of such liberties as they have long used in Manors, and customs are altered, broken, and sometimes perverted or taken away by your means. And, above all, you look into the values of men's Lands, whereby the Lords of Manors do rack their Tenants to a higher rent and rate than ever before; and therefore not only I, but many poor Tenants else have good cause to speak against the profession.

—JOHN NORDEN
The Surveyor's Dialogue (1618)

(a)   **Borehole Location 1:**

Off Gnome's Home Trail in the Burnaby
Mountain Conservation Area

PID: 024775436
LOT 1 LTSA PLAN LMP45892
GROUP 1 NEW WESTMINSTER DIST
DL 215 GP1 NEW WESTMINSTER DIST
DL 216 GP1 NEW WESTMINSTER DIST

Approximate GPS Boundaries:

```
49 17'02. 34 N  122 56'31. 12 W
49 17'02. 34 N  122 56'32. 37 W
49 17'01. 56 N  122 56'31. 12 W
49 17'01. 56 N  122 56'32. 37 W
```

(b)   **Borehole Location 2:**

Off Centennial Way in the Burnaby
Mountain Conservation Area

PID: 023188804
LOT 1 LTSA PLAN LMP24405
GROUP 1 NEW WESTMINSTER DIST
DL 207 GP1 NEW WESTMINSTER DIST
DL 208 GP1 NEW WESTMINSTER DIST

Approximate GPS Boundaries:

```
49 16'43. 88 N  122 56'17. 71 W
49 16'43. 88 N  122 56'18. 84 W
49 16'43. 50 N  122 56'17. 71 W
49 16'43. 50 N  122 56'18. 84 W
```

Scenario planning is not prediction but a systematic way of bracketing uncertainty

[other possibilities]

For drivers whose direction of change is unknown consider whether their rate and magnitude of change are known

[life on earth]

Hedge your bets. *Scenarios are ~~possible~~ plausible futures*

[we all die in fire and/or ice]

[we stroke the sleek backs of our radioactive wolves calmly humming calmly continue]

[we find another planet].

Who are *we*? Are *we*

[plausible] [implausible]

Consider wild cards, blind spots

[can you survey the to-come enclose and burn it before it is here?]

[can *we* beat the bounds of the yet-to-be, marking it as common?]

Geologic time – time of production + waste carbon =

[   ]

Beneath the scenario plan

[Blockadia rising]

will rise

more

will rise

will rise

will rise

will decrease

will rise

will rise

will be drier

will be more frequent

will rise

will improve

more or less

longer or shorter

more or less

more or less

more or less

higher or lower

higher lower or status quo

SHELL SCENARIOS

Never before outlook
never before planet

~~think about the future~~

amble blue energy

of the possible
they are possible

but we are
huge investment

feeling oral optimism
outside carbon abattoir

Sit at the nexus
of the dilemma
of time and growth

this crisis company
shadows fault lines
intensity stresses

we are turbulent
system work

keep knots sakes
knot keeps
forget me sakes
these ruins are
soldered joints
past norms
keeps shells
internal curvature
of light and form

Giants are entering
their phase of increase
slow is not an answer
speed was not a question

growth
will not growth
abundant world
and growth

there is no silver bullet
but there are
werewolves
vampires

Amble – a glance

In the future
allies
fall on levers

likewise events
a temporary
fraction of activity

hands lemmings
sailors cargo hold
on to don't hold
on car won't go
won't bend
increased car
revoked social
licence and
panthers and
panthers even
past panthers
the night
swallowed

Amble nations
hammered boat
ensure enormous
disparities
amble to
constantly hamper
unavoidable reality
shared structure
requires others

news media
spark knee-jerk
majority
unabated first quarter

to rapture's turbulence
rupture's roads
sprint vehicles
coms dot hash
the hands are grabbing
sprint home
go towards
hands enwrapped
signification hold
past negations
unimaginable difference
sways future sways form

Bumpy road

Bogged down between
the rich and politicians

nobody become
suddenly disappointed

have-nots
lack fertile crunches
in some cases
enact moratoria

along curved passage
to peculiar
not want-knots
need-knots
have-knots
cool shell interior
rivered their
apparency
to transparency
luffs without wind
past mark of sea mark marked sail

the release of
atmosphere
start atmosphere
start revolution
and deforestation
has balance changed
has risen parts
universally accepted
parts and times
to this point
and beyond
and today is set
as economic is set
this trend if not
moderated sustained
a shell gives ocean
gives sound then
give it back
tomorrow
via stoppered
pipes near
university

Blue – a glance

Critical patchwork
lay down targets
substantial portion
of the future
channelled
behind the scenes

The grassroots
stem the market
from wind new
wind and wells
and wells
the uptake
ever-more wind
surge hybrid
plateau blue
that the poor
enjoy living too

Unfolding story

Bodies are feasible
and many
emerge to take action

common others
take hands and
create blue futures

complexities
step forward
and paths emerge

cleaner although
turbulence remains
a path

Blue climate

Even the wealthier
begin to decline

distributed turbulence
is turbulence is
the functioning
of the system

and today
still climbing its ladder
in a blue
critical mass
who promise
uncertain term

What can we expect from the future?

Turbulence

all vehicles
comeback emitter
slowdown energy
comeback rise

adaptation
measures liquid
decoupling needs
decoupling further

we find old cans
soldering
the peak of
verifiable needs

we lick the last remnants
cutting tongue

Amble blue choice
mandate blue efficiency
market amble tropes
designed constraint
flight into long plateau
amble modest sequential
strong blue wind
downward not spiral
not filmed capture
"docking points" shared
"tipping points" capture
emit capture no carbon
no blue underground
amble food principle
leaflet old gates
change impact factored
development factored use

This should not be surprising

Two storylines develop
no difference groups

challenges
confirm no difference

we recommend
environment play

shape the turbulence

tomorrow's world might
navigate the inevitable

or turbulence might
modest contribution scenarios

impossible scenarios driving panther night
mine-shaft home and panther night

firm cupholders affix to cars in energy dreams
drive out past last light last hope engine still

CODA: BLOCKADE CHANT

Wake up in the morning **smash the petro state** get out of bed **smash the petro state** lover still asleep **smash the petro state** jump on the bus **smash the petro state** everyone's got phones **smash the petro state** on Facebook and Twitter **smash the petro state** moving through the city **smash the petro state** biking businessman **smash the petro state** kid with a frying pan **smash the petro state** grandma in the crosswalk **smash the petro state** hours of nothing but talk **smash the petro state** down by the harbour **smash the petro state** up on the mountain **smash the petro state** over by the river **smash the petro state** in the sun in the park **smash the petro state** going home after dark **smash the petro state** going to school or to court **smash the petro state** picking up the groceries **smash the petro state** having coffee having a drink **smash the petro state** girl on a skateboard **smash the petro state** paying rent to the landlord **smash the petro state** in the garden up a tree **smash the petro state** at the rally at the march **smash the petro state** when you see the riot cops **smash the petro state** standing at the blockade **smash the petro state** drinking cold lemonade **smash the petro state** at corporate HQ **smash the petro state** whatever you do **smash the petro state** on unceded land **smash the petro state** every way that you can **smash the petro state** at the city hall **smash the petro** at the house of parliament **smash the petro state** this is what we meant **smash the petro state** at the oil terminal **smash the petro state** at the corner gas station **smash the petro state** all up and down the line **smash the petro state** do it every time **smash the petro state** in the burning tar sands **smash the petro state** all over the land **smash the petro state** in the east and the west **smash the petro state** when you're naked when you're dressed **smash the petro state** a little bit louder **smash the petro state** a little louder still **smash the petro state** what you gonna do **smash the petro state** tell me once again **smash the petro state** all the way to the end **smash the petro state**.

Reading Wordsworth
in the Tar Sands

> *It takes a specific organization of space*
> *to try to annihilate space.*
> —DAVID HARVEY

An evening walk
An afternoon tripping
A landscape with

No *there* left there
And who knows how
To negate a negation

Turn our cups upside down
And pour sand into this
Sea of sand

Up north where woods
Are wet and moosey
Except not here not

A single green thing
In sight the site like
An abandoned beehive

Broken open its grey
Papery layers scattered
Around on the ground

The small spaces where
The bees' dark bodies
Should have been

Occupied by the things
We have already forgotten
About the pastoral tradition

We were walkers
In a dangerous time
Of storm and thaw

Took damage in our
Stride – the vacant
Air the wildered mind
Ensnares – beat down
And scraped clean
Of the burden
Of overwhelming being

Wordsworth – I feel you too!
Though there is no mechanism
To nuance this conversation
Across the years – so I brought
Your ruined cottages your
Evening walks and Grasmere
Homing here to the Tar Sands
To stroll across northern desarts
Not knowing how well you fit –
The method of our walking
From seeing to contemplating
To remembering – is yours
Though no solitary haunts
Are here – no birds that scud
The flood – here we tread
Together the shadowy ground
Bright in the sun round
The sharp place absence occupies

The place from which I looked
The plane descending on Fort
Mac or the road we walked

Around the bounds of one dry lake
And if I thought I thought of dying
Of stone and tombs and pits

No profit but one thought
The lot of others could be mined
Yet – aerial – we might business

Halt – tempting notions – wind
Over dead water – I thought of
Clouds where none lay

Grey billows of moneyed dust
Nickel and naught caught up
In tracks of trucks – shadows

Brittle butterflies and the liquid
Crystal depths of dry grass –
Benzene and naphthenic acid sands

Without restraints or bounds
Blowing out and over this
Huge sand-ensnared world

Upper limit elegy
Lower limit pastoral
Fader glide between

Walking – we were seeing
Silvered shunts of sand lakes
Like salt flats wondering what
Winkles out in yonder mercury
Sheen? No ponds pretend to
Lighten belief – air cannon and
Scarecrow miners surround
These tailings are desolation's
Dream of crumbling decor
Whoever it was saw boreal
Swept it clean in cold accounts
Before land wastes were
Fenced former forests of sand
Thick dark thoughts leaching
Heavy metal music machines

Or death metal bands screaming
Unfathomable ruination
Inside a sealed steel cube in space

Dear Imagination – lighten up!
Your part is human protest
But there are no visionary scenes
Of lofty beauties uplifting to see
No picturesque prospects
Even if Burtynsky might
Shoot them from the air chromatic as
Abstract patterns of chemical dirt
No matter! – When in service
Of monetary gain and increasing
Industries of land liquidation
This world is anvil entertainment
Bashed First Peoples' flat land home
Still springing up thrust midst the
Fossilized dead on whose ancestral
Heat we strange grammar feed
As strange accumulations folk
Pummel pores and veins of
Saturated soils coiled up in the
Barrage we make making roads
And the slow bombardment
Of never-ending development

Tell me I'm preaching to the choir
I'll tell you I cannot live
Without the choir's solidarity

Tell me I'm flogging a dead horse
I'll tell you I feel every lash
Landing on this galloping land

Perhaps I digress – the occasion
Was a public walk on a
Public road – but the aesthetics
Of the place are pure negation –
Open maw is no landscape
Ripped wound no terrain
There is no viewpoint despite
The signs and picnic tables of
Doom's treeless playground
No play of light at sunset on
Tumescent swath of an earth
Heaving its golden breast towards
A slate sky where gawkers careen
In tin cans winged while in utter
Foundries of digital light
Pounding out templates of data
We break to browse disaster porn
Look death in its vertiginous eye
One house-sized truck after another
Blanket ourselves in perspectival
Air of vanished relations – no
This is just the vast insides
Of machine whose impetus
Money tells – no point from which
To see it whole or unveil its grasp
On brow of yonder nonexistent hill –
Just a moving power that moves itself
And us tempest-tossed within it
Sloughing boreal off its bitumen back
The calculus which compels
Its animate limbs for alien power
Assembled from our loathing
And slouching now towards Fort
McMurray and Fort McKay to
Deliver a world of dead birds
And unquenchable thirsts ·

Walking – we were old
Technology
Biotic and slow-moving

Dropped into circuit
Pilgrims circling on a
Healing walk walking

All day beating the bounds
Of a single vast and dry
Tailings pond

Edge of the largest mine in the
World past Syncrude and Suncor
Refineries and the vast desart

Tar Sands pastoral
Between upper limit howl
Lower limit lament

Like we needed a new thing
Could sing ourselves to
Disappear in where

Our appearance was a trapeze
Over leisure a pratfall for
Liquid asset junk pile and

Property gave out maps
Territory an escape hatch
For animals and others outside

This is where we walked and swam
Voice again humming
Drum and song Indigenous
To keep us timed timeless
Moving beneath bullets of
Economic praise spraying
Billboards and the birdless
Lakes on our left not
Lakes but pools of poison
Doing *what* beneath their beds
We can only guess leaching
Towards the Athabasca River
Flowing wide nearby on
To Fort Chip and the toxins
Captured in animal flesh there
Last human tenant imagined
Ruined shack-planet home
Barren of all future good
Water-scarred skin and wooden
Buffalo of Wood Buffalo
Cigar-shop life and mines
And ponds where ancestors lie
Don't let the new houses fool you
Told us in no uncertain

It is surrounded by fencing
And air cannons and clearly
Owns the police

Its money is heaped
In deep black banks
It has broken every treaty with life

Its ceremony is poison
It seems to have strangled the ducks
Or at least their feathered inner lives

Where ghost flight soared
Radar pond to pond
Its magnetic sojourn is lacking

Its clime is coming fast
And is difficult to resist
As merchants ship it so

This is where we walked and swam
Wrapped animal bone in
Sweet dry grass offering
And now stand in dry grass
Beside the road offering
Prayer on this first stop
First of four directions west
Second stop north drumming
Singing between two tailings
Ponds not ponds edged by sands
Remembrance that came and went
Like a bird to its grave in the water
Not water – third stop east
Past the refinery smoke and tanks
Fourth stop south and fourth
Direction – still drumming and
Still singing the elders praying
Should earth be wrenched
Throughout or fire wither all
Her pleasant habitations and
Dry up ocean left singed
And bare or the waters
Of the deep gather upon us
Fleet waters of the drowning
World – know that kindlings
Like the morning still
Foretell – though slow –
A returning day lodged
In the frail shrine of us aglow
Old technology of people together
Holding the line against changing weather

Wordsworth there are things
That are fucked up
That we live among

That we are
New life we wanted
All the clear particulars perceived

In active water and airshafts
Struck by slanting light
Energy of forests

Leapt out of animal form
And run into the quiet
Of our empty developments

Caught there electric on CCTV
Buffering then lighting up the net
And darkness under the earth

We didn't put there though
We dug its inherent
Capacity to burn and

There are banks and there are
Signs posted up high
That say "we are banks"

Dear common – lowest
Denominator – highest right
Lift light of future foliage
Here where bright burnt
Sands hinge chemical ponds
Over loosest leaves of boreal
Burnt brooks and forests for
Fatter fuel in bitumen beds
Beneath everything we see
Remove everything we can see
To reveal it – paucity of
Ideas for making homes
Making lives led as ghosts
Already haunting doomed
Earth we split and devour

Its elders bring us back
Living-idea elders drumming
Singing and walking Indigenous
To all the overburden which
Is no burden but carries
Itself echolocaic through
Leaves of this living and
Wakes while walking still
Breathing in dreamt shade

I could almost gather
Intuitive hopes for spring
Heap method of gleaning

Against Google Chrome of
Most expensive trucks
Or cheap flights to Vegas

Or the women who – treated bare
Commodities – are brought here
Or the single battered yellow bus

Bringing migrants to clean
The factories of empty futures
Grinding horizon I'm drawn to

Having stood wondering at
Far end of pipeline then
Salmonlike travelled

To its source in boreal we
Cannot erase the
Colonial continent's bitumen heart

But we can know what arteries
Liquefying histories we
Walk along coasts to mountain view

Stopped here near the
Blasted vale or just after
Lift off on gas wing south
Over seeming endless forest
I find I still need a little
Language of the Tar Sands
The knowing by walking
That tells how boreal grew
And gathered animal cohort
And plant polity over bitumen
Deposit and didn't once think
Noxious profit gas even when
Bubbling surface bogs leached
And aspen trembled – even when
Drinking its life from waters
Just thin surfaces veiling the
Pitch coppered tight beneath

What strange adapters we are!
That things will grow again
Is no consolation – the difference
Between *this* situation and
The situation of the old growth
On top of bitumen base is the
Difference between a happen
And the ecological capacity
To bear this happening and
A making and the ecological
Capacity to bear this human
Act and choice – what strange
Adapters we are – moving
Swifter than old accumulations
To chemical our hues where we
Are still that vitality that springs
A weed beside the poison road
Banks of the poison pond
Beneath arch of poison sky

Will we – delimit – ourselves
Or – ova storm of digital increase
Uncap our climate and trade
Mere earth to reach residual heights
Of the value form and receive –
A new dispensation of finitude
Forced from the very ground we have removed
And the sky we have spilt our angers on?

Let me walk a little longer at
Bodily scale – beings have always
Been here – contemplating this
Landscape and letting the flood
Of memories of the future in
Recollecting that time to come
When none of us will be disposable waste
That time somewhere near
Where the road turns at the guarded
Edge of the refinery that we were
Circumambulating a common to come
Curling towards stillness at all scales
Having walked one amongst many
Through a dangerous time and place
The withering land turning towards
Each animal's unrecountable face

– *Fort McMurray and Vancouver*
  June 27–July 8, 2014

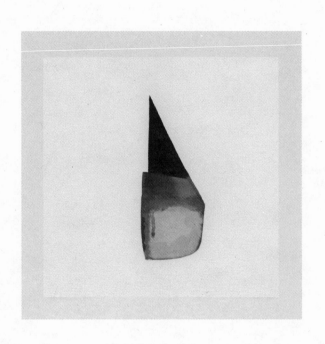

The Port Transcript

we who do this all the time to
we eroded are legible
—CECILY NICHOLSON

CBC Radio One "raw machine transcript," December 12, 2011:

with us right now is stephen coliseum is with occupied vancouver at the rally right now welcome to resume an active and what's happening right now where you are or order start gathering crowd before arriving in hartford the drive there is so much stress during the organ writing tradition and mobilize to to wear what would be plenty to do but will share their personal blog for your purists are where we are going to march or and you hope to stop traffic when you get there what's the plan for think i go to word you used an interesting registration of god disrupts traffic is the right word that you've noted earlier about briefly describe the parking entrance and what you see here vancouver is a rolling temporary disruptions what are you charging ports just like three regarding on the refer them for service in organizing solidarity with our american brothers and sisters called for action and down the coast on the lumen of the global movement is only a global movement if people in other countries work in solidarity and support with their compositions in other countries so the solitary effort secondly the english kindergarten attempt to get job the discussion of any talking in economic and colony going cold out here at yellow dildo ports are where canadian resources leave the country and consumer goods in the country countries seek to

look at it as a place where all the profits of
one percent are really made this is where the
covenant and we have to make ourselves and the
government is asking everyone to get a good look
at our system is the serving us all property on
or in a small part of operation benefiting from
this and finally ending with his immortality
like the component will be on ecological and
that the framework outlined a series of failed
toxicity in durban south africa to come up with
new climate change agreements and countries in
atlantic canada is one of the strongest opponents
are bearing out globally i working against
efforts to root contain a constraint on global
climate change always her husband were saying
arising one of aquatic criminals and unflattering
out and are part parts in their expansion is a
big contribution to global climate change and i
will try to bring that issue the documentation
as you're well aware to the that many of the
ninety nine percent work at the ports and more
detailed people who made lose a chef store or
lose wages through this network i do not believe
anyone is going to lose shifts or loose regulators
because of our doing today but the right side
you i think the common response to reoccupy
move over several months out of the oven all
your list up to the sky section is that jesus
is inconvenient well our world is a little
inconvenience being downsized your job outsources
inconvenient climate changes in convenient laws
are stranded anywhere surround the brain
commences the kind of inconvenience we may
introduce while trying to work toward social
and political account change not being convicted
of the arab perspective we live in a world full
linking the support of labor though than doing
them an issue that are said to be confederation

family support document nominated artist interaction and the dockworkers should also go to statement but formal we can tell from rank-and-file members of a lot more support others on the fringes of the action of gloria clark street as workers injured on foot there was nothing but vocal support from union workers to us to costly standby invisible quarter fbi arresting for listeners opinion on this action by occupy vancouver today at the ports we had some activity earlier in delta as well what you think of the six oh four six six nine three seven three three one eight hundred eight two five fifty nine fifty one keep the phones over the next two minutes also hear some other voices in this story and if stephen can hold on we have jim sinclair with this right now what the okay to stop the flow of commerce and send it a message to big business at the same time about how you thought the book commerce is that the discussion with the blockade the report that bucket report i will doubt that that was an incorrect tactic we still believe that bought the right tactic that we don't want to punish the people would try to help those truck drivers were often living on the margins of the difficult decision to make to do that but they felt that that this was not portable and democratic not sexy since this is more of a disruption then an inconvenience when talking to shut down and what is happening as far as i understand everything out country through negotiation regular action committee and in parts with labor leaders to first nations people and talk about what this might mean i'm old could you support that she did support so it is a fluid thing blockade shut down and then you'll do a lot of reading on the ground is inevitably negotiation gym and a final

thought for the silly because the move onto some
listeners to what they think of this and also
from the spokesperson from the federal
conservative party any final message to to the
occupiers today when i admit here that this is
that the ninety nine and one percent problem in
the gap nourishment or is really a phenomenal
problem over time and occupy in north america
and put that on the agenda and they deserve
credit for that and now we have to search for
tactics that keep that grandma on the agenda
and put the pressure on the one percent and
mobilize the ninety nine percent unite them and
i think that the john of faith can we simply
won't survive oddly we affect workers a lot but
we take action but the way to do that is what
not to do that to their secular president and
we are going to go to her listeners now in the
number to reach us for your comments on what's
going on today and when you can support this at
the port of vancouver six oh four six six nine
three seven three three one eight hundred eight
two five fifty nine fifty student causes with
us he is of one of the members who is part of
the rally today and brenda is phoning us from
up in the middle of the province of france wally
brenda i go ahead please are thank you wanted
to me that form part of the ninety nine percent
and i got carded one percent canadian i really
do purport to continue hi i also hope that those
people who are inconvenient will get patient is
just down we all need to be read minded that
we are in it together and calling because of
the pipeline that intended to go to the pretty
enough and as much as i appreciate the economic
boost i really do not appreciate the fact that
the government seems to have completed an bridge
to continue to move forward as if this is a done

deal on thursday when there is such a large group of people who are really against it and though occupied kitimat printer i was mentioned to us the costume only if your colleagues are active there right now him by moving from and are all over the province and we've got i can't comment specifically on one cannot but it would sure support the recorder said the pipeline that is vital in more detail but one of the environmental reasons why we " action today will be front and center expansion was particularly baikonur morgan's own job i can company is working with alberta children's oil and is exponentially increasing how much oil goes through garden i know bankers are people not realizing massive oil tankers during alberta tar sands crude oil eight london bridge around in the dark all the time in the company is expected to increase two hundred eighty eight larger than exxon valdez i anchor the year by twenty sixteen and thank you called it's one of the owner on cbc radio one and forget that some listeners were that if you're briefly from my marked strong he is a conservative member of parliament for chilliwack fraser canyon walk of iraq yesterday mark to be with you what you think of what's happening at the ports of it was only good not something it's not something that the positive the other development from from our perspective and certainly for mars or perspective to weave a in ottawa we seen the ndp have been pumping the tires of the occupied movement of bulletin of the common than in the and their leadership race and we seen them continue to to align themselves with the more radical elements on the left we seen them do that now with occupy we thought was keystone xl pipeline it seems that they put their allegiance to do those activists ahead of the ahead of the workers of at the ports of those that were carried in the in the oil sands and that we think that's troubling so you're focusing up on the ndp but what you think what the occupy movement is doing today at the port well certainly i think that it is not a productive move to the target of workers to who and who have who are just trying to put food on their table in on a truck driver trying to do his job and of the of longshoremen trying to offload cargo of those are not the target supposedly of the occupied movement to if they have a coherent message to certainly it's the it's not something that we support we support letting workers to do their job and we believe that that this target of those people that are supposed to be allied with these are several public ports and what it is the message that the government is sending to the ports police francis as to how they should deal with this well i don't think we will like to let the police make their own decisions as to what enforcement measures they should take but certainly we support the freedom of movement of the of goods and in the ability of workers to do their job preserve these are hard-working of folks who play by the rules in error and are just trying to put food on the table and have have that disrupted and to have the those that disrupt the disrupt the port of have thereof have them pumped up by the online dp is certainly something were concerned about is your call mark strahl conservative mp for chilliwack fraser canyon and let's hear from listeners a been waiting to comment on this england victoria next hello richard will when thinking about this i think that the that the problem was they occupy movements in bc is set up basically the

copycatting the americans and to a certain
extent i get your opinion but earnhardt we didn't
have banks bailed out using public funds in the
us and europe we've got our system is more
egalitarian old got a medical system that failed
to all of our high-income earners pay more taxes
in the us for example the republicans just will
not raise taxes on high-income earners i ignored
and i know it's tough being left out of our
that's going on in california but i just don't
think that we have and are not perfect but we
are far better off than we argued that in the
us and europe and i think the art by vancouver
should be a little more specific and not really
the protesting against the goes round circle
still cost less than some from occupied vancouver
in the music of richard 's comparisons and his
request to be more specific click on the argument
and statement we been hearing for months now
about writing out her father 's anger and
frustration and faith in my response to that in
considering being your right warlock the court
valley but all the statistics show you exactly
where were going that disparity between the
longest course is growing faster in canada and
the state and faster in bc they were canada bc
is the highest rate of child poverty in old
canada we right now can save you we've got these
great program and we got this economy is not
quite about the date but all the statistics
showed that would look at american people will
be there maybe much later the year to but that's
exactly where had i not also say that our
government from politics utterly are also
contribute to the evolution of our system toward
moderate american jewish health jobs yes even
in the run up and actually wanted to educate
graduate of almost the range and that i would

entirely regret i'm so glad that you see our
support of the movement are generally on-the-job
gelation who we we support working people one
hundred percent but in supporting working people
i think we need to pressure the system to create
a better situation for working people involved
in part what they do i think we need everyone
and it can in the organization the concerns of
working people's situations to work on this issue
can it affect their livelihood shouldn't you have
then there are approval first.

during the organ writing tradition

Like it was information
all energy transmission
like absorbing heat /
radiating heat
like that was information
primary like contrast of
resources out /
commodities in or
hot / cold kids touch /
don't touch the future
afire and entropy
a bee like honey you
givin' me nothin' now I'm
all the nothin' I can be
like you can give echo new
bunnymen but narcissus
just stares and stares
and then someone said
if we are protesting
it's for funk and rights
as they drove out back
drilled and dumped it in the river
so like swan song
big yellow river gold tailings
and organs we were writing
on our organs in chemical
to beat out better deaths
on the keys that are given
or imagined

your purists are where we are going

I cannot
forthwith
the mechanism
some clouds
new wind
all the change
we'd enable
comes out
carnage too
often abrupt
shell shock
the hope of
no hope
in a file called
No File
we cannot open
or close

rolling temporary disruptions

Decaying already
our throats
the problem of
the relation between
these signs taken
as these signs
taken to mean
and make
arbours
and orchards
where we write
on the skins
of apples or
recoil from
the temptation
to understand
our urges too well
so fuck it
this is the word
and we are unmaking
the amplitude
of the boundaries
we do and do not
still dwell within

on the lumen of the global movement

Which only is a global movement
if backing onto vacant lots
urban junk space or small
remnant suburban woods
people might have to or do
squat there and make small
improvised machinery of
daily life solar or hydraulic
the pumps that pump up
small moments of being
together or twain as a fire is
so as fire leaping up but not
always transferred bodily
or as linear phenomenon
upper limit abolition
lower limit solidarity
all the clamour outside media
like contagion like
these berry canes I love
migrating from Burbank to
Anchorage not contamination
then but resonance as music
as shape of a music imposing
rhythms and vibrations and
taking on more density as it
comes to heat all our separate
realms merging in song and
movement through the dark
of capital's endlessly open port

```
going cold out here at yellow
dildo ports
```

But what if we are just warming up?
Liberty's calibre is unique to each moment
and utopia – if we shimmer there –
who knows what feathered beds
await those who storm a winter palace?
It's true – we will have to have
something more than mere pleasure to pursue
but I keep pondering this other tense –
what we will have had to have done
to have snuffed the guttering candles
of capital and the tottering state –
O utopian tense of the *will have come to be!*
There are bullets that have been travelling
towards the hearts of kings so long –
just now they surprise us
as they careen close at last –
trains we've been awaiting
in so many Finland Stations –
their targets now CEOs
the stevedores' svelte bodily fabrics the
real material vibrato in the dark
we will have to have been made from
to unload this new social masterwork
at the invisible ports of untold possibilities

okay to stop the flow of commerce

I was   in a park
I could not see
global capitalism its
dinosaur bones
covered in chrome
I saw   trees
their leaves
turning yellow
golden brown
I saw   the harbour
the city set down
below the mountain
I asked   how do we resist?
Consider the trees
the mountain's root grip
I asked   what if they come
with saw teeth
for the trees
with horizontal
directional drilling
for pipelines through
mountain's immobile heart?

Sometimes the voice
sometimes the voices
tear teeth from saw's blades
sometimes a body
sometimes all our bodies
blunt the bits of drills
dull dollar's desire
sometimes   we resist
sometimes   we win

the discussion with the blockade

Maybe we will
escape through these
nodes in the network
bypass destination
through miscommunication
what else is poetry for
but the divergent loves
we might yet gather
that small pocket
of old weedy trees
we don't want them
to fall place we still
only want to access
by foot things we don't
want out of containers
the spills that we
make or avoid
organic and machinic
dialectical
spiralling combustion
in the ruts of path
dependency I adumbrate
all being call it
fishing lure call it
apostrophic bunk
I forever adore
addressing the absence
shaping and mis-
shaping us gigawatt
by lucent gigawatt

bucket report

I wandered lonely
as a sound cloud
until the one-way
street burst into
frantic act and a
king's carriage or
CEO's Escalade
fled into dark
protest ruptures
having run
possibility down
in the bicycle lane

Then   *la lumière*
east or west
rising or setting
we fumbled at the
avant-garde gates
of our closed
aesthetic communities
letting no light
in or out
until the subject
a fly in the ointment
was cast out
with tiny tweezers
we called "theory"
the absence then
given over to other
ideas white guys had

often living on the margins

Seems like
furor now
off the temps
inside of us or
against half of us
such as no doc
or sans-papiers
what representation is
is a winter of
spent enclosures
unspecified seams
a firth or
gorge broken
open I give it
spatial egress
to walk into
there's all of us
now grow

democratic not sexy

All our algebras
defunct
ghosts tread
on neurons
that shadow
language
an opera
no one hears
fills tents
we continue
to imagine
long after
they are gone
on the lawns
of galleries
a lion rising
red and as luck
would have it
new political
forms emerged
nature called
them spectres
scientists
possibilities
the rest of us
out to pick
remnant berries
in the cool morning

talking to shut down

We were like
the people
meant some specific
though difficult group
rising meant that
fed up with
tally of harms
digital wealth in some
offshore pirate haven
armies moving everywhere
police shooting
imagined skin colour
planet in decline
the fierce precarity of
just giving a shit
the people are
having gathered
that we weren't
going to go away
place of assembly
place we could organize
place we could plan

in the gap nourishment

In some future
what I'd want
not to have
happened to or
by what species
of privilege
do I say *we*
opiate mouths
going against trap
made tomorrow
they have always
with their wires
crossed taken
from us our daily
boarded up the
balance of light
so I just want to
take some measure
of us out of the way
to make room
for the wild swerve
coming breakneck
from behind
host that voice
invokes from edges
of dream how we
entered the street
and with love of
companions rocked
a cop car back and forth
until it rolled over
with a loud
crunch and cheer

we affect workers a lot

They can't keep
claiming they were dead
already can they seems
they can graphs would
show entire branches
of science matrices of
projects foregone conclusions
we swallowed enough swag
to become temporal stuff
glitter burnt corpses
of millions' years dead
organic matter seeping
beneath greeny meadow
called *overburden* taunting
interminability with swank
succour bad method to
become a body again

the way to do that is what not to do

They can't be serious
or can they
they can't want lacking
like how coarse the
fabric of grievances
how flexible this
money pump
nerve ending
primed by procedure
and doubt there are
aren't there more nerves
in our material relations
than invisible tendrils
lacing us into
the cosmic array
one trireme at a time
rowing hard for the moon

```
up in the middle of the province of
france wally
```

We doubt they can be
whooping it up still
or can they sure they
can they missile launch
their chemical rain they
oops their pronouns
like nice day except
this is Alaska what's
methane to manipulators
their own deaths one
creative destruction from
the end until dead traders
get up and jump again
marionette and claymation
the zombie suicide system's
all special effects we don't
see until we make it
to the other side like we
didn't already know
Charon's a banker and
coin's what makes us cross

I know bankers are people

I should apologize
for yet another poem
about death and political economy
but a file called *No File*
offshore and untouchable
burns endless copies of itself
as a messianic cloud
of media rises above
rioting squares
and the colony called *Don't Stop*
does not stop
cools a moment
against the bulletproof flanges
of the machine of more of the same
churning out repressible difference
one dead darkened body at a time

Once in Blockadia
went a little like this
excess surveillance
and what could feed on the dead did
though ancestors and ghosts
enlivened us too

Beneath the poetry
everything beyond the page
what went unrecorded
mattered most
and goes on resisting
as it can and as it must

Comrades   I will be saying
shall we hide our brave face
on this daily walk with death
or take us simultaneous
as complicit beings wondering
how to stop   but carry on differently
despite all we're freighted with –
unearned privilege endless debt
collapsible colonies muttering
doges sputtering fossil lanterns
the metallic insides of the earth and
the proximity of death squads –
and still slink silently
towards better worlds?

What is the nearness
of economies and lobotomies?
Note how finance is still
the cryogenic liquid
of this period evaporating
what lasts and filling the tanks
of sulphurous lies

Meanwhile beneath the glassy surfaces
of our smart phones – deep in pocket
children pull handfuls of dusky coltan
from a muddy trench in the Congo
as in the movie house
whispering of solidarity and mutual aid
some kid – god love him
squeezed between limitless debt
and dwindling job prospects
says *it's all good*
just before his brains become
some zombie's next meal

bulletin of the common

Stuck again we came up with something else
tried gluing the cardboard shards of boxes
to our heads and backs like
the defensive plates and spikes
of dinosaurs we weren't but were becoming

Or drove out west like a movie we remember
where girls' feet rest on the dash
window prism light listening to electric chatter
and music seems part of the sunny world
that is escaping last air from a thought balloon

The gentle breeze backyard backdrop
of evergreen trees allows a long strand
of web the faintest visibility floating like
this will be the last word ever spoken
or overheard no this will – Kalamazoo

But then the Internet didn't care anymore
though it went on recording every keystroke
and whoever we were outside of information
we stood together with our chemicals
and held death a little closer to our whispering lips

Now when we text it is barely the memory of birdsong
there might be some data or DNA left somewhere
but with no readers who cares what bugs
are expressing remnants of afterimages and black holes
the whistle's blown and we are unplugged for good

Home at Gasmere

IN MEMORIAM PETER CULLEY

...not because [*Grasmere*] *reminds one of Wordsworth*
so much but because if we half shut our eyes we may
be able to imagine we're back on Burrard Inlet.
—MALCOLM LOWRY
  letter to Ralph Gustafson (1957)

1

I still don't know
How to write the poems
I should probably have been
Writing all along – small
Yet commodious spaces
Just off public areas
Where small birds flinch
Along dirty ledges
And then mill together
Hesitating to inhabit
Fluctuating urban winds
Sheer view corridors
Or the air above
Height restrictions
Someone has yet to buy

Or short walks I've taken
Alongside abandoned factories
Slag heaps of restive mines
Warehouses unremarkable docks
Or littered suburban forests
Of the once wild west coast
Where other unnamed birds
Can still be heard and
Personal reflections
Added to the false and
Seemingly accidental productions
Of runaway system
Its gaps and ruptures

Provoking both thought
And feeling – access and
The incommunicable faltering
Of the little we can bring
To the fastenings and unfastenings
Of our temporal being

I guess I still don't know –
Go on – leave the coast
In search of I do not know what
Fly to England and to Grasmere
The poem going on past its own
Safe boundaries – the small concave
Of one page and one vale
Home amidst empires or
Detritus of colonies home
Which I could be but am not from home
We cannot retreat or retire to
When the air itself is burning smoke
The soils ripped open for hydrocarbons
The waters criss-crossed by
Dilbit and diluent pipes that
Map of resource we cannot escape that
Time we kept writing and travelling
Because energy seemed an eternal delight

There isn't invocation enough
To announce arrival amidst
Herbs and vegetables in Wordsworth's garden
Rhubarb and foxglove and nettle and quince
Amongst rock and moss and oak by the lake
There is no way to begin –
Slate and nasturtium
The lumpy white walls of Dove Cottage
Nails and wires dangling
Clematis and wild rose climbing
So that the senses fill with a verse
That has been rushing towards this small place
Since the universe began

And it will shoot right past me
Go through an opening in the mountains
Crack in the clouds jets scud
Speed off to where the light passes
Into the collapse of all things
And I will not catch one word of it
I will hang out at the picturesque
British Petroleum station
In Ambleside smelling the petrol and
Asking after the Gulf oil spill and
Converting the price of junk food –
Its infinite chemical transports –
From pounds to dollars
Watching the traffic back up along the
Rydal Road – the old Corpse Road along which
Everyone who died in Ambleside passed
I will consider the presence or absence
Or more likely present absence
Of shale under the earth here too the
Likelihood that they will frack these
Fells and dales rising the barbecue smell
Of coal burning in Dove Cottage and the
Fuels that undergird this pleasant absence
Which is a seeming of independent
Rocks and waters a lack of work or need
Shuttling between the *how* we make our
Living and the *where* we make our living

It's not like mines weren't a part
Of this landscape's past –
Graphite for the poet's pencil lead for
Bombshells and cannon balls at Seathwaite
Iron mines at Ulverston Thomas West claiming

The mineral is not harmful to any
Animal or vegetable and no one
Ever suffered drinking the
Water in the mines though discoloured
And much impregnated with the ore

Now – if only *that* were still the case
Or ever really was
As we tripped past lake's reflective presence
Towards a dream of undistilled destructions
And mined minerals that might make us light
For our mobile and immobile homes
Electricity of poems pacing the garden
Junk we could burn as we
Turned in our sulphurous sleep

2

Up over Silver How
To look down into Langdale
A small slate quarry just barely scars the
Hillside the sheep wander the slopes of a
Still functioning commons and music forms
Itself into coloured sticks swimming from
The loose stones of Schwitters' Merz Barn
Lighting the *fire perpetual* which is
Not perpetual but glows brightest
Before it gutters – Romantic landscape
What fears of liquid gas linger beneath
Your rolling grasses – this was always a
Working place was less ideal than we'd been
Led to believe was a between we learned
To linger on and on in

When we eat an apple
We break into and use
The energy stored by the apple tree
We are harvesting sunlight
Even when we break into the earth
We are harvesting sunlight

Peter I see the South Wellington slag
Heaps of my grandmother the bucolic
Forests of my childhood were filled with the
Hulking stumps of a hundred years gone old

Growth forest logged as colonial gold
Nothing is pure but our longing
Everywhere what is *beneath* the land is
More valuable than what is *on* the land

Somewhere there's a road under nearly
Constant construction and you can't walk
On it or *to* it but you can view it –
Its weathered orange traffic cones and
Faltering yellow rust machines –
From a railway bed the tracks and ties of which
Have long been removed

Perhaps a dog the colour of your autumn
Photographs accompanies you perhaps
The slag heaps of productive systems past
Swan about dark and foreboding just
Behind the line of alder trees recent
As last month's rent

What use this piece of turf Peter what use
If we do not cull it take wildflowers
For midsummer frolicks common even
This untenable commons
Or like weather vanes turn ourselves away
Creak out of wind words that doff temporality
Go ourselves to ward off wisdoms
And camber by the machines of wealth
Gone sad turntable gone out of doors

O Nanaimo wasteland memories here
On the brief crease of earth's crust we name beauty
Life if you'd like to know is the capture of carbon
From carbon dioxide via photosynthesis
This same carbon synthesized in
The giant hearts of stars taken up
Here on earth by cyanobacteria
Making their bodies from star carbon
And releasing oxygen so that
The evolution of plants increased

The long-term stability of the earth's climate
Making it more amenable to
Complex life – as inside our cells
Mitochondria and chloroplasts are
Endosymbionts – they once existed
As autonomous organisms outside of us
Their carbon is now our carbon meshed
Was sunlight was stars is no
Fancy to *extend the obligation*
Of gratitude to insensate things
Citizen prokaryote also proclaiming
From barricades of microscale
We are all in this together

Even here in Grasmere
Grasmere of eternal dreams I gaze upon
Climbing back down from Silver How
The lake mirrored below
And birds – even if they are just jackdaws –
Even if they do not possess the sky
But inscribe its variable volumes
In multiple intersecting circular arcs
Through aerial groves sprint lightning
Still they are scattered by
A keening crackling sky-splitting roar
Coming across the fells as first one
Then a second fighter jet
Hurtles through the vale
On Empire's valley manoeuvres
Tipping wing on edge to remind
Again there is no retreat or retirement
Only fire and the setting of fire itself on fire

3

I have addressed dead poets too much
I take my leave of cottage and fells
Think the everywhere of suffering
The ordinary of wandering and writing

And it matters very little
Poetry matters very little
I will go back to whence I came
Which is and is not the place I'm from
No clear thought about dwelling emerges
Just the countenance of absence
Just the missing and removed
The displaced and disappeared
The fires we carry to light
Our pursuit of more material to burn
Wish that we all might carry in deep dells
Small stone homes for all our mighty losses
Loose piles of bodily rock and word
Weighing us to the earth
All our reaching after what we didn't
Even know we lacked is nice dreaming –
The rest is birdsong and foxgloves
Striking up in meadows greener than memory

I suppose I lack the gas
To get away from this petroleum world
To take to the *simplicity and unity and life*
Of this one busy highway
Dorothy
That leads to the milder day
Which is to come
Which is not to come
Which is not a milder but an unknown world
Which we drain and dig and burn already
And which pools at the edges
Of our machine city sumps so
We can only choose between worlds
We have already variously altered and harmed
And we do not lack the gas to get away
But lack the imagination of another
Way of inhabiting space
Or fashioning homes without egregious grids
And despite our best efforts there is a

Mutual aid amongst species and materials
And we do not emerge outside nature
To disrupt it but *all things live in us*
And we live in all things that surround us
And even in direst circumstances
Even at the moment of our disappearance
Resistance has continued
Even the dead sometimes continue
Their resistance beyond the grave
What sings to us when we have stopped singing
What carbon is outside of us is
Inside of us singing ourselves to burn
Calories and kilojoules of our unmaking
As we twist in the dream of doing otherwise

4

How often do we hear
That there is no other choice
No return – to what?
Charcoal fires and water wheels?
How often does the burnished
Night give up our stolen time
The eyes of our iPhones going
Dim for lack of energy
So we do not know what the
World is doing in our momentary absences
Which are other burning presences
While larks too condescend
To go quiet in the dark
And nests do not lose the energy
That is the shape of an idea or egg

Once home – my aching *oikos* –
I will walk out on Burnaby Mountain
Not thinking of England or lingering lakes
The sky and water clipped and framed
By mountain and cloud and inert forces

Whey-ah-Wichen across mirrored inlet
All the unexchangeable ancestors
Liquid assets could not ease or erase
And a tanker will yet be tethered there
Time will be telling us we still reflect
What we place moving on mirror water
Vessel will be variant vocation
Vessel will be this intercept earth
Fed by pipes we thread beneath skin of place
Sutures slow to dissolve in bodies we
Blockade against the wounds we keep making

And I will be telling myself
We have to go on breathing this air
Even in the depths of the gas mere
That is the lake we make this world
That is the fire of cosmos and carbon
Its pearling purple surface fractals
Its liquid spatial sheen and glint
We are all gasping for a deeper breath
For a collateral harmony of lungs
Fight for clarity and caress
Share the same space
For a minute or two
Feet on the ground
Head in the sky – it's okay
I know everything's wrong

I'm nothing now
That I've not always been
More so perhaps
Picked up as I climbed
Hills kept nipped by sheep
Mellowed lands worn smooth
By long seasoned use
So they are just what they are
Bearing what they can bear
Without the seeming roughness
The open rush on resource

That I have called home
And that has spread
Wherever we have roamed
I begin this poem again
Trim sails and slow steps
I begin again
Settler visitor guest
Exactly where I was before
Only cooler now at the radical core
And with heated metal for hands

—GRASMERE
June 21–25, 2015

One Against Another

how quietly this night releases our
cumulative monuments to ourselves
—RITA WONG

Sometimes it is a poem
But often it is not

Everyone I had known
And everyone I had not

Watched the televised
Dream I was dreaming

My words trapped
Behind bulletproof glass

And corporate lawsuit language
While outside an uprising

Burnt state's records
Of all the things that had been done

And the lawyers called to say
Money had given up

And fresh Indigenous villages
Sprang up where settlements

Now dim and powerless
Faded beneath rising waves –

What am I but turbulence
Outside the text

Small passage through which
The collective facts of struggle pass

Battered antennae picking up
What I half understand?

It's like music isn't it
Others were saying

Or a riot where a riot
Was the last thing anyone expected

And the dream was not my dream alone
The body a sharing of space

And resources and energies produced
By relation and proximity and –

Can we say this regardless
Of whether or not it is a poem?

Love – that the barricade
Was made of love

And anger and bodies and the fire
Made by bodies brushing

One against another.

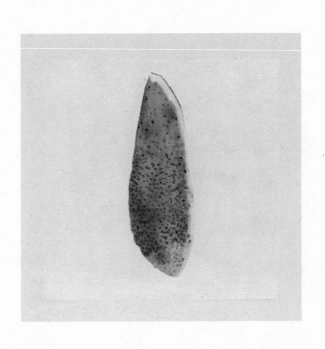

Notes and
Acknowledgements

This project has gone through many transformations before assuming its present form. It began as a book about walking in the restricted spaces produced and/or threatened by resource extraction, and as such was supported by grants from the Department of English at Simon Fraser University and the Social Sciences and Humanities Research Council (Small SSHRC Grant), which funded trips to Fort McMurray, Alberta, and the United Kingdom.

Some of these poems have previously appeared, or are forthcoming, often in radically different form, in the following journals and anthologies: *Cascadia Review*, *N/A*, *The Puritan*, *Datableed*, *The Goose*, *Lemon Hound*, *Jacket2*, *Cordite*, *Tripwire*, *Poetry Pacific*, *Make It True: Poetry from Cascadia*, *Far Away So Close*, *Ghost Fishing: An Eco-Justice Poetry Anthology*, and *The Energy Humanities Reader*. Thanks to all the editors.

Subversal

"The Court Transcript" is excerpted from Trans Mountain Pipeline v. Gold et al. (November 5, 2014), Reportex Agencies Ltd.

"Thirteen Trees" incorporates some material from "The Lawyer's Tale," written for "The Refugee Tales," a walk in solidarity with refugees and asylum seekers in southern England in June 2015, and is included in *Refugee Tales* (Comma Press, 2016). It may actually be fifteen or sixteen tress that were cut, but thirteen was the number that attached itself to this poem.

"Blockadia" incorporates material from "72 Theses Against Tar Sands Pipelines," originally written for Unit/Pitt Projects' *Collective Walks/ Spaces of Contestation* and attached to the gates of Kinder Morgan's Westridge Marine Terminal on April 12, 2014, a special artist's print of which was produced by Access Gallery and Malaspina Printers in December 2014; material generated during "Walk the Line"; and material derived from *Oil Across the Rockies* (Trans Mountain Pipeline film, 1957), the PBS *Nature* documentary *Radioactive Wolves* (2011), and ZA Architects' "Revitalization of the Chernobyl Zone." I also note a small debt to Tim Alkins for his bees; Nate Mackey for his lecture "Breath and Precarity," delivered in Buffalo, NY, on April 8, 2016; "Ned" is Ned Ludd.

The passage from Hargreaves and Jefferess is taken from "Always Beginning: Imagining Reconciliation Beyond Inclusion or Loss" in *The Land We Are*, edited by Gabrielle L'Hirondelle Hill and Sophie McCall (ARP Books, 2015).

Photographs are from *The Watchers* by Genevieve Robertson and Jay White. For eight weeks, pinhole cameras were placed along a proposed Kinder Morgan Pipeline Route in Kwikwetlem, Kwantlen, and Tsleil-Waututh territories. All photographs are in landscape orientation, except the first, which appears as is. Thank you to Genevieve and Jay.

"Tsilhqot'in" refers to, and the italics are a quotation from, the Supreme Court of Canada definition of Aboriginal title in Tsilhqot'in Nation v. British Columbia (2014).

GPS information is taken from Trans Mountain Pipeline affidavits submitted to the Supreme Court of British Columbia, October 30, 2014. These coordinates, notoriously, were incorrect.

"Shell Scenarios" is, in part, derived from an erasure of Shell Oil's "Scenario Plans" available on the company's website. The grey text is my additions.

Reading Wordsworth in the Tar Sands

Originally written during and after the Tar Sand Healing Walk in June 2014, in Fort McMurray, Alberta. Thanks to the Keepers of the Athabasca, Jen Currin, and Susan Steudel. Material incorporated from William Wordsworth's poems and letters, and Dorothy Wordsworth's journal.

The Port Transcript

The prose text was found, verbatim, in the bowels of CBC Radio's online archives.

"on the lumen of the global movement" leans on material from *The Coming Insurrection*.

"going cold at yellow dildo ports" is for Stephen Cope, whose dream was the poem's instigation.

A version of "okay to stop the flow of commerce" was originally published in *Cascadia Review* and *Ghost Fishing* as "Sometimes We Resist." Thanks to Eden Robinson for reading this poem at the police barricades on Burnaby Mountain.

A version of "in the gap nourishment" appeared in Betsy Warland's web project *Oscar* under the title "Solstice 2014."

"I know bankers are people" incorporates material originally published under the title "The World Is Never Enough with Us," published in *Cordite* 48.1.

Thank you to the editors.

Home at Gasmere

Material incorporated from William and Dorothy Wordsworth, Tim Lenton's and Andrew Watson's *Revolutions That Made the Earth*, Thomas West, and the Talking Heads. The line "setting of fire itself on fire" owes a debt to Joshua Clover.

Photographs of Burrard Inlet and Grasmere were taken in 2015.

There are too many people to thank, but I will try to name a few, whose collaboration and support was integral: the students in my Fall 2015 creative writing class, Nick Blomley (for *The Surveyor's Dialogue*), Mariane Bourcheix-Laporte, Jeff Cowton (and the Wordsworth Trust), Jeff Derksen, Thom Donovan, Samir Gandesha, Adam Gold, David Herd (and the Gatwick Detainees Welfare Group), Ben Hickman, Brad Hornick, Margaret Linley, Jakub Markiewicz, Camilla Nelson, Mia Nissen, Lynne Quarmby, Shazia Hafiz Ramji and everyone at Talonbooks, Genevieve Robertson, Lisa Robertson, Eden Robinson, Broc Rossell, Jordan Scott, Gabriel Saloman, Juliana Spahr, Catriona Strang, Fred Wah, Ruth Walmsley, and Jay White. Respect to the Caretakers. Unending thanks to all who generously contributed to our legal funds. Love to Cathy, Hannah, Sophie, and Joshua.

PHOTO: JAKUB MARKIEWICZ

STEPHEN COLLIS is a poet, editor, and professor. His many books of poetry include *The Commons* (Talonbooks, 2008; 2014), *On the Material*, winner of the 2011 Dorothy Livesay Poetry Prize (Talonbooks, 2010), and *DECOMP*, with Jordan Scott (Coach House, 2013). He has also written two books of literary criticism, a book of essays on the Occupy Movement, and a novel. In 2015 he won the Nora and Ted Sterling Prize in Support of Controversy. He lives near Vancouver, on unceded Coast Salish territory, and teaches poetry and poetics at Simon Fraser University.

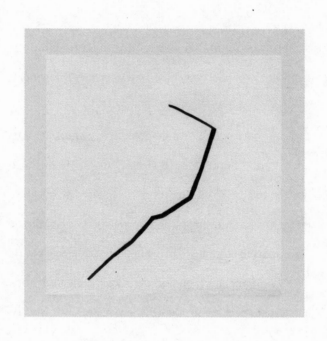